D1456551

Heart Attacks

Frost to Skellings,

Skellings to Frost, it's difficult
Across this dark. I remember, of all things,
Your tie, conservative, with a little pattern,
Tight about the neck of a boiled shirt
Sharp with starch. Everything matched.
And your thin white hair combed forward
In a residue of vanity. That night
You couldn't eat before the reading,
But got down some egg custard.
We had our picture taken. The bright
Flash burnt your old eyes and they watered.
Then you leant to my ear and whispered,
As if it were the inside of your soul,
"The bastards are killing me." Oh Bob,
I went on after you died, but never
Righted a wrong. It's been a long time
Since you took my arm and mumbled almost
Under your breath, "It's a big step."

—*Edmund Skellings*

To Louise

Heart Attacks

Edmund Skellings

A Florida Technological University Book

The University Presses of Florida

Gainesville / 1976

PRINTED IN THE UNITED STATES OF AMERICA

Library of Congress Cataloging in Publication Data

Skellings, Edmund.
    Heart attacks.

    "A Florida Technological University book."
    I. Title.
PS3537.K33H4   811'.5'4   76–17593
ISBN   0–8130–0557–4

Contents

Heart Attacks

Incantation

I keep coming to this chair
Today. Back and forth between
The ficus tree trailing aerial roots
Outside, and this chair.

Back and forth between
The tame wood and the free.

I am a hammock hung to the winds.
I am a sail today.
I strain as hard as I can and then
Go back to the measured tread again.

What can I start? My pencil breaks.
The ficus creaks with the breeze.
The chair creaks with my weight.

Axes, I threaten. I shall kindle
Some kind of blaze. You shall be
Food for fire if not thought.

The empty tree whispers of singing birds.
The empty chair is silent with its dead.

More, I shout, to the arching rafters.
The door shudders on its jambs.
The shelves under the books stiffen.
The table offers coffee.

Oh God, I hear the forests falling.
Timbers moan in the holds of the ships,
Spars sing in the wings of planes,

All the toboggans in the hills are rushing,
Skis are hissing,
The great woods of the world are howling.

The pines of the walls encircle me.
The polished years are shining like brown bones.

I sink into the chair.
The tree enters the house.

Now all the druids are dancing.

At Sunland Training Center

After hearing a poem read slow
About snow
And holding the scraping
From a freezer
Melting through her hands
The mongoloid child says,

Snow is like wet pants.

We are aghast. Not only
Has this child thought, but
Made her own poem. Yes.
Snow is
Like wet pants, and we

Who have learned to walk, talk, not
Wet our under things

Wince at the arrogance
For it is not reserved to kings
The arrogance of our own
Power.

How fine and up right we are!
Only occasionally knocking
Things over, only once in a long
While tongue tripping.

Superb and splendid,
We chase the world well, only
Twice a month perhaps
Crying over spilt

Lives. Oh my, we never
Dreamed that we would finally
Know it all.

The child looks up again
And says so we will not forget,

Snow is like wet pants.

To His Machine

Are you still here,
Black thing of terrible teeth,
Humming and clacking?
Deep in, a developing growl.

Let me say
Your parentheses have ever
Been only part of the circle.

Some day all your asterisks will fall.
You'll end up in business
Or back to school.
Your numbers will be up.

Good riddance.
You have always been
Stingy with exclamation!

Dash it all, be kind.
And not too questioning.
Spell my name right and one night
I will free your carriage,
Release your margins.

I will buy you a red ribbon.

You can go and
Shift for yourself.

Crown

There is a spot
On the back of the head
That body and self spin round
And go down.

This is true. Ask
Any demographer of cells
And he will nod.

Some men go bald
There first, and some
Later, as emptiness
Creeps up from the eyes.

All of us know the spot
By feel, and I for one,
Confronted by questions
With no sides or bottom,
Reach up and rub.

It is some
Sort of answer. Rub.
Perhaps. Rub.
Maybe. Rub again.

At least we have found
The point of
Mystification. From there,
Who knows?

The Double Helix

I

When I am a ghost
Do not believe
In me

Believe
This blackness curiously lined on white

Interstices of thought and breath
Believe

Intervals in the struggle of the heart
Believe

This
Believe:

That a wild curve lit my mind
Was
Perhaps my mind

Retinal shadow of the surface of the world
Panned gold of the camera brain
Slits of the senses mere slits

Oh saddle shaped light
Oh inky rider

II

At tension
One thought in the chamber
He killed his dream

One simple idea he took
From no book
Put it to his head

Pulled its trigger

Fact
It spoke

And so he woke

III

We all rode many times
On the ole D n A

Up from the swamplands
Out of the sea

Ho ho honey
You rode with me

Now that you're here
All that behind

Down from the branches
To see what you find

Fear for your body
Hope for your mind

We all rode many times
On the ole D n A, et cetera

IV

Spun thing
Center of all sun thing

Wave of space

Galaxies like fish slosh
In you

That's a new twist
Said Mother Matter

E is M times me some way
Figured Light

Strain
Said Culture

No Yes
Said Brain

I am a sine
Origins pass by

That Time
Is running in

V

Woke to a code

IMPERATIVE CONTACT SELF
IMMEDIATELY FOR FURTHER
INSTRUCTIONS STOP

Woke to a call:
It's me. You know. It's me.

Woke to this
Believe

That the white bat universe flies
And we ride its winging

9

In a wild curve in the cell
In a wild curve in the night

Know says the cell
What says the night

And the helix twists of infinity
And time is the turn of the twist
And the spine stems and the fingers leaf
And the eyes flower

Oh saddle shaped light
Oh inky rider

Fictions Personal

"My right side is masculine.
My left side is feminine."
               —patient to R. D. Laing

You caught wise. Your truth sticks out
Like a sinister thumb.

What do you know of directions
In the twist of the genes,

The curvatures of the chromosome?
What do you know?

Insiders, those eastern meditators
On the Yin and the Yang,

Felt cross sections of all spines
Sunning their selves

Like cats arching. Or palms spinning
So slow only a seed could

Whisper wheres. Well, you caught me
Up. Strong as a Lear ramble.

Only thin covers separate our stories:
You next to me on the bending shelf.

Prices

Each year
The cost of paper
Grows more dear.

For you,
My Jewish printer says,
A deal.

He is full of inks
And watermarks.
His fat thumb riffles a ream.

This ought, he winks, to
Hold a poem.

How can I answer every
Poem is a raw
Deal,

Each word of the way
Illegible, unruled.

He cocks an ear to the press
And with the nail of an index finger
Tightens a screw one turn.

He cries to his devil,
Trim this even, then
Come back this evening at eleven.

All this while
The press is shouting,

Similar similar similar.

Up North

Here comes Summer with a bird in her throat
Sings some dumb poet from New England,
Who has waited the winter for a piece.

She *lives* in Florida, mate. You're only
Another fling. Who know her well tell
A whole other tale. Remember this, john,

She catches cold easy, begins about Miami,
One day a nip in the air notes a loss:
She'll take all her clothes and the hifi.

Get wise. She'll pop her dime down on
The ponies at Hialeah, lay herself
Hot on the beaches, follow the dogs.

I know you think you're a slicker,
Not a drop of naive left in the bottle,
But don't bug *me*. It was you got your hopes up.

Yerkish

It was all right with us
When they painted and people
Paid money to take home
Ape art. Money is
Partly funny any way.

Garish blotches with
Little control reminded
Us of our own art
Attempts. Disorder
Makes humor, goes
The equation. Who
Could ever get those
Long brushes to work
Right any way.

This, though, sets
The teeth on edge,
Apes garrulous as
Hell, chatting with one
Another, make the
Heart chill. God
Will most likely
Be brought up.

What then, any way?

He Says She Says

She says it is
A cinch. All you
Have to do is

Get on your toes
And turn. But when
I do I can

Feel muscle stretch.
He says one must
Limber one o-

Ver the other.
He says it is
A snap. I think

Near that word, too,
But do not speak
It in my head.

The book says don't
Struggle, but here
Even was a

Trouble. Who do
We do this for?
Do they think God

Is loose? Think His
Great joints will flex?
They say it's all

Matters of the
Posture. Let them
Go hang, thinking

Eli! Eli!
Surely something
Inside will give.

Oval

I am given a gift.
A butterfly and a flower.
A metaphor framed on a black oval.
How fitting.

I put it under the lamp's light,
Shining and artificial,
Trophy of some afternoon
Of love perhaps?
Or summer boredom.

For a moment I can feel the caterpillar
Aging and drying.
Colorful creature,
Have you had enough of dying?

I do not know, blue and brown,
What you are.

Let someone else call out your name.
Your name. Name.

And suddenly I am pressed, too,
At a thought of Yeats

Spreading magnificent wings.

Social Security

We argue, my father and I, about
Economics, though he calls it plain
Money. All are at the till,
He complains. "They"
Took everything good away.
Politician means on the take.
I, he says, worked every penny shiny.

Here, mother comes through
From the kitchen,
Her eyes raised significantly
To heaven.

Dad, I say, using the word
Fashionable when I grew up,
It isn't that way.
At seventy five you already
Have back more than you paid.

He says, I make them pay because
They made me pay. It's justice.

I say, the numbers of elderly
Have increased, thank
Modern medicine, and . . . But
I have brought up doctors,
A bloody mistake.

Those butchers, he shouts,
And my argument collapses
Like a vein.

Once long ago, before
Even any of my poems remember,

My father put his hand on my shoulder,
Which was going off to college.
He looked me in the blue eyes long
And said, Go learn more
Than your poor father.

I did, Dad. Does it do any good?

Conventions

Mr. Gravel uses vitalis,
Or at least looks as though,
And he's a Senator, U.S.

I watch him on the tube,
Supporting native rights
And a supersonic airplane.

Remember, Mike, when I flew
Us around Alaska, the big
Rally in Nenana, that Eskimo

Covered with blue and orange
Buttons and drunk on your
Whiskey? When I asked him,

With a small grin on my face,
Who will *you* vote for?
He answered, Ralph Rivers.

I said, What the Hell
Are you doing with all
Those buttons for Gravel?

He said, They make good
Fishing lures under the ice,
And then he had the grin.

We've both flown a long
Way since then, Mike, but
Often my brow crinkles.

Who attracted more fish
That season? Who tugged
Their hooks into nature tighter?

Crossing the Doral lobby
In Miami, you said, *You
Know, you're in show business,*

Too. I thought, then, of all
The speeches. And that orange
And blue lure, spinning coldly.

Treasures

Gramma came to the sunshine
State, brought by her daughters,
The blonde, the red, the black
Haired one. Away from the old
New England roots, now
Mouldering like forest mulch.

She sunned and hummed and then
Her mind began to slip.
One day they came upon her
Weeping for nothing. Why,
They fluttered, why?

My pretty box, she cried, with all
My treasures, gone for good.

But there was no box.
Later that night they learned
Her sister died away that afternoon,
The younger, the one she always
Took care for.

Not given to odd beliefs,
The daughters smiled.
An odd coincidence. Odd. Very
Odd, was the most wonder
They would own to, being modern.

Today that day came back
To her red haired daughter,
Now gone gray. And this gray
Head, my mother, tells
Me all of it. Tears, like little
Bifocals, help her read the past.

Long after she has left me
To myself, I keep my eyes tight
Till colors swarm. A pretty
Box appears. The lid is ajar.
There is nothing in the box.

Hemingway

Never quit
At a spot suitable,
He told us.

When he knew what
Would happen he
Put down his pen
And leaned back safe
With a head start
On tomorrow. Then

Was taken care of,
Characters
Frozen happening,
As if the film
Broke.

One early morning,
Sure what was next he
Got up from his life.

The Leningrad Writers Conference 1942

for Yevgeny Yevtushenko

The starved had reached one thousand a day
With the temperature thirty below zero
And the writers had to burn their chairs
But they did meet and hold their conference

Zhenia, tonight I watched the old films
Of that Hero City holding out holding out
Holding out under months of shells falling
On homes with thick frost on the inner windows

And I thought of our first meeting in Alaska
With all the writers gathered at the college
And how we talked of poetry half the night
While outside the cold and the blackness waited

Zhenia, tonight I sit writing in Florida
Sipping from the simple white of cold milk
While the long breath of the air cooler
Settles over my shoulders like a shawl

And I hardly know what I am trying to say
Only that somehow the boiling heart
As well as the frozen bone must be held back
By poets who must ever keep their conference

Memory

Oh, these paper
Flowers are faded.
Though they did
Last a year
The sun got to them.

Man knows no dye
To fix forever.
Glass slowly goes.
And stain in woods.

Your words
Had sorts of colors
Once to make me
Wonder.

I'd hold them high
Long after they were
Over.

They have weathered so
I cannot tell if they were
Ever
Sweet or sour.

I rush to your photo.
Yes, the face too is turning
A little yellowed.

Now I am forced to flush
All old thoughts that were
Enamelled.

And see whether.

Remembering Mailer

Provincetown:

After the afternoon sail
On the publisher's catamaran
We got ready for the
Big Party at Norman's

The sail was calm enough
The party loud enough
Drunk enough

And then they all went home
Telling stories

There was only one fight for
You to get into

One boy lay on the porch
And cried

We sat with the last
Half bottle of warm bourbon
To watch the dawn
Raise over Provincetown

Then everything was still

I praised Yeats and you said
I can rewrite anything
For the better

I opened the book
To one of many
Turned down corners

You said flat
I'll be damned if I don't

Well,
Damned if you didn't

Then we were silent, too,
Over what had just happened

And a huge fireball
Rose from the water

Another Oval

Hair soft about her oval face,
She says, You don't talk
Right in a poem,
I mean, a poem goes
Different.

I answer, Tell me
More.

She says, hair tossing
Soft about her oval face,
It just, well, like, it
Sort of dances.

I answer, Let's dance
Then.

She says, Oh you.

An Archeological Site in France

This find this dig will last them years
Hard by a cliff where once a river ran
Melt from the foot of a glacier now
Perched on the top of the spinning globe

Thirty students of assorted sex
Living together for two summer months
Under the direction of careful professors
Casually dine beneath their canvas tents

Each day unearths more evidence of men
Much like ourselves in stature and in aim
Though in a colder climate under a harder sun
But now the students wash and clean their teeth

During daylight the sable brushes work
At bone and flint uncovering bit by bit
Layer under layer under layer of those lives
Revealing masterpieces of conjecture

Even the cigarettes of those who smoke
Are delicately stubbed and pocketed
As well as paper wrappers from chewing gums
Or tissues from hapless students who caught cold

They eradicate each hint about themselves
At the end of a day labor before
Precise cameras wheel in and align
To document the tight terrain they work with

And slowly the remarkable portrait grows
Of how the culture called cro-magnon man
Mated and hunted and played and died
And because it shows his soul made art

30

Some mornings miraculous discoveries
Hard and clinging clay is scalpeled off
And as old as Genesis sculptured in bone
A white ten thousand year old mouthless face

Two necklaces have so far been disclosed
Whose rawhide thongs have long since disappeared
Each shell and tooth together in location
That makes mere chance position beyond chance

That same day found ornate abstract engravings
Whose meanings are entirely unknown
Although analysis by a specially set computer
Implies the nicks make calendars of the moon

One professor having turned the finds for decades
Offers these non-industrial people might have
Painted and carved and inscribed pictures
Purely for entertainment in the winter

Two giant elk of course by now extinct
Are represented in one totally fine example
Which uses the cave rock face itself
To emphasize the muscles of the elk and ibis

And one wall painting rests at the far end
Of a cave within a cave where the painter
Must have lain with his right arm extended
As far as he could reach with a long brush

It is completely in the utter darkness
And the man or woman must have brought a fire
Or else have traced the animal outlines
Without ever seeing the finished features

Which shows how intimately the artist
Knew the anatomy of the animal or else

There may be some perfected explanation
That lies beyond our knowledge at the moment

Hair seems to have been quite important
And braids of every sort adorning statuettes
Are rendered in exaggerated detail
As well as the usual giant phallic features

The flint tools that were used for carving
Can even today be made by patient hands
And an old professor with time to kill
Has imitated the production of an axe

We might even postulate a shrine
In an area far back in a particular cave
Creatures half-man half-beast exist
Proving they had a certain imagination

Red ocher with which they brightened statues
On ritual day may still be found in crevices
And curlicues upon the little figures
Although the form of the rites are not yet clear

Some shapes are very obviously totemic
Meant to gather power for the hunter
In order that he be more than a match
For any angered beast he might encounter

One enterprising painter used a natural hole
Already present in the rocky wall
As the eye of a bison in full run
And the eye even now seems quite alert

New questions promise clearer answers
And we can only wonder what they may
Have chipped and carved from the blue-green ice
And set up in these caves to worship

Animals life size and larger
And also beasts we have no record of
That peopled their primitive lives and thoughts
Smoothed into miracles by their own warm hands

The students often let their minds so roam
About the valley after the evening meal
While the professors read and happily argue
And the same style continues at Lasceaux

Extrapolation

Most of us is math, which comes as no
Surprise: The limbs of trees circle
The trunk, leaves the branch, all
Spin slowly the great tap root. This
Can be seen from palm frond about
The nut, arms and legs popping from
The spine, twinned brains blooming.

Go down deep and you hit math. Every
Time. Darwin shaped it up by
Statistics. A natural arithmetic.
He stopped there, but because each
Poem should have one great idea,
Here: Extrapolation is genetic.
That should account for you, big eyes.

Naturalist

This peaceful lake
Of Central America harbors
Such odd creatures

As the Yellow Spinesnake
And you see him now
Upright on lilypads
His yellow hood spread
Like a bright umbrella

He feasts on the pad frogs
Catching them midair
At the exact top of their leap
But now you see him
In the strange erect
Twining of mating

For all the world
Like a medical wand
And there hops

Andrew's Lacewing
A very intelligent bird
Who can swim with his wings
And leaps
Out of the water for

Now in slow motion

The giant dragonfly

And remarkable for a bird
Builds his nest half under water

With rushes and watery weeds
Giving birth to its young live

And here you see the Brown Rockfish
Who backs into caves and crannies
Expanding himself till his mouth
Seals open the opening
And then he waits for
Minnows

Each of these remarkable species
Eats its own young
Which is common
Only at this lake

Perhaps only in our time

History
May look at us from these
Camera angles

Too and find
Our camouflage wanting
Under its infra
Red

Science Fiction

Take an animal almost extinct,
A huge hairy beast that, threatened,
Gathers his young in a circle,
Facing outward, for all the world
Like a herd of soldiers surrounded.

Suppose this animal intelligent enough
To dig through deep snow for grasses,
Bright enough to slide open doors,
Lift latches to escape from enclosure,
Loyal to companions of other species.

Imagine a man. Taught to love money
And automobiles and girls and all
Else Americans hold dear. Imagine him
Of good stock with a fine inheritance,
Married to a woman of impeccable looks.

Imagine him educated in finance,
Economics, the history of cultures.
Imagine him suddenly choosing the Greeks
Over the Romans, suddenly spending
His entire fortune to capture the animals.

Suppose he suddenly sees,
With his mind's eye, Man as another animal.
Suppose he barely glimpses, at first,
As heat waves trouble the vision
Of a field of grasses, that all

Animals are equal. And, for a moment,
The man sees with the eyes of the sun.
Suddenly all is simple, his life clear:

He will domesticate this beast,
The first for a thousand years.

Yes, that would be a story,
If we had a man like that, a hero
Of only his own battle. Picture him
Large, with massive features, picture him
An American with a mind of his own.

Simplify the scene. See him and the herd
Facing each other on an infinite plain.
Hear him talk low to the animals,
Then soft to himself, "I will find
The right men to take care of you,

Men almost as extinct as you,
Who will care for you as they
Care for themselves. Who will never
Touch your meat. Who will pull fleece
For weaving the lightest down clothing."

Picture that and you have my story.
Imagine him finding those natives
And taming those beasts, and see,
At the last, the bond between man
And animal so tightly knit

That the animals protect around him
As they do their very own.
Ask yourself if you are not moved
By this portrait, somewhere beneath
Your heart, behind your postures,

Behind your lies to yourself that
There are no men like this, that
The story is impossible, that

No one would write a tale like this
With his whole life. I will not argue.

I will go aside and read from a book.
And if you do not believe in books,
I will bring you North, to the edge of land,
And show you the great dark animals grazing
And the natives carding their wool.

Epilog

for my friend John Teal

Blunt, bluff handed, he
Can be accused of
Having befriended animals,
A silly vice in such an age.

Add to that.
Unpardonable sinner, he
Has also befriended Man,
A foolish flaw in any age.

But he goes on and odd,
And it is no surprise
That in that way
He has befriended God.

From the Striped Chair

It has arrived again,
Caterpillar season, only
This year I do not get the
Broom, sweep cocoons
From the screen, tidy
It all. Instead,

I swig at the half
Bottle of vodka left,
Let the world spin.

This yellow one, I
Spy on him from my side
Of the plastic veil.
All is insect green
And perfect, he
Thinks. Mouth
And mouth, something
Tells him, and it
Will blossom right.

I know that call, heard
It young. At least
By the age of
Reason. It did, then.

But I tell you, bundler
From the sun, truster
In future beauty, that
Won't do now.

Sequel

One day past my warning,
Friend, and in an orange
Flash, you are plucked
By an oriole.

Too soon flying,
Food for chicks,
How is that deep slumber
Now?

If it comes, let it be
In our sleeps,
Dreaming of a tomorrow
Lovely in color,

All sex and wings.

Amulet

Wary to keep
Front hooves from the mud
The young buck at the waterhole
Has already been singled
By the yellow grasses.

The grasses watch him drink,
A nerve in his neck flicking.
Quick, the antelope jump
Running and gone.

The lion leaves the carcass
To lap some water. Then she drags
A path in the grasses.

I watch from a spot
Even more secret. I will scratch
On a small stone a hoof
Under a tooth
And over both

Power bites fear.

Surface Tensions

The blades of the wooden oars leave
Circles in circles,
The water parts at the prow,

These are strange waters.

What prowls, terrible and terrific,
Brooding?

The light line I cast in the night
Tremors, tugs,
Goes bottom in a whine, the twine

Smokes, the boat
Dips,

And line boat and man go under.

Who wins in this fishing?
We struggle in the dark,
Lung and gill gasp,

Element against element.

I nail a huge trophy on the wall,
Wet and dripping.

Look how his jaw mouths teeth work
Slimy inaudible words.

Listen to how old his sigh.

His drowning is my poem.

Grizzly

The Toklat grizzly
Is so smart
You end up being hunted.

So much for smart.

Boulders, thick brush,
Anything to conceal
Our motives.

Guess again.
There are some things
That stalk our world
That will not be put off.

They have the scent.
Step lively.

Tout

Here
Give me a leg up

Thanks
Now in the fifth
This is a good filly

And in the eighth
Top Spot is your best bet

You know
Gave my last wife
The same tip yesterday
She won't go for it though

After a while you can tell
The people who chance it
And those who pick

The favorite to show

The Elbow Room

A riotous old fellow
Came into the bar today

He said chief the job
Is getting *to* me

I need to use the pay phone
Call up a girl I know
Or something

At forty three
You never know whether
The old engine
Will kick over
Cold mornings

Got to stay in touch

And these hours
Are doing me in
All day hanging walls

Why in hell this sudden
Privacy? If I had my way

There'd be no more
Partitions give us

A beer your honor
Give all of us
A beer these wages

Make a man think

Home Made Candy

Pride first I suppose
Or perhaps
Names are a sort of spell
Put on a product

Aunt Jemima's
Duncan Hines'
Howard Johnson's

Then as the business grows
The name dwarfs the man

Imagine having a cake
Named after you
Or ice cream melting

Not at all like a statue
Or a bridge to somewhere

Not at all like an automobile
Though that's getting closer

And no nickname will ever stick

Dunc Hines or Howie J. won't do

Nor does Mr. seem appropriate

This naming and claiming
Must go on I guess

We all want to get up in the world

So I have recently decided

To place on the roof of my house
In at least neon

Skellings' Red Hot Poems

[The red hot will flash on and off]

Shooting Match

Suppose one day you find yourself
Against the wall or a post
Hands tied behind and blindfolded.

Just suppose. And say
The resplendent officer offers you
A puff on a cigarette and you don't
Even smoke.

Or say he gives you a last few words
Which is extremely unlikely
But you have nothing in mind
Except nothing.

This is of course only supposition
For really they put a black bag
Over your head.

Up till then they tell me the condemned
Can't take their eyes off the pistol
To a man.

So you never truly get any last words
Unless you lie in bed and even then
Most times nobody listens.

For actually dying is a living hell only
For very literary persons who like
A neo-classical neatness.

Who prefer their symphonies finished.
Life tidy. No poem ending in
And . . .

The Hartford Circus Fire

A poem recalling the great fire
of Ringling Brothers Circus in
which hundreds of children were
burned to death. This ended the
outdoor tent circus in America.

toward the construction of mystery:

Al, the Phoenix, who each matinee
Lunched on coal and kerosene would say
This should have been his tale to tell. He'd bitch
If he grew hoarse and someone did his pitch.
Al never tumbled to the gift he lacked
And tried to tell the truth about his act,
As if the real were wonderful. The fact
Got him a small house. Then, burnt, he burned.
Confusion was a truth he never learned.
The last time that I looked, for once, his eyes
Were bigger than his stomach. Al went wise.

If you'd be barker for yourself, begin
Most carefully at pitching your "come in!"
For some will call all circuses a sin.

toward the construction of entertainment:

Small seats. Oh how we packed them in.
Not since Obadiah and Old Bet
Have towners crowded to the till to get
Their folded spieled away. Hearts lost within,
All else was given freely, for the lights
That glittered in their minds from sequined tights

Spun sweets on which imagination fed.
The eye was almost pipered from the head.

Small seats. While each one counted elephants,
We counted cash, and sunned our skins with dreams;
In floral winter quarters, warmer schemes
To round out a rich season with the tents.
We had a fine blue sky that no cloud crossed.
We glowed in our desires. We were all lost.

clown white:

The tumblers had gone off, when smoke
Rose, and a cloud
Of laughter
Rose immediately after.
An old joke touching a young crowd:
A flimsy house, a loud alarm, a shriek.
None of the clumsy volunteers could speak.
Hysterically falsetto, one throat screamed
Oh save my child!
The red truck rang its bell and then went wild.
On rubber feet, with giant toes,
And gripping tightly his prop hose
Stood spotlighted and fixed a man
Who was a clown, whose features ran.

cage:

Behind the booted man who claimed
There was no beast he hadn't tamed
A yellow mane of fire roared.
He spun, thrust to those jaws the scored
Rungs of a painted stool
That kept a hundred cats in school
Then like a fool

Forgot his rule
And ran, but Oh the sawdust floor was slick
And Oh that licking cat was quick.
He fell. And the stiff whip
Went limp and melted in his grip.
Down fell the planks. The flames flew up.
All at once his blanks blew up.

rope walker:

Above the crowd,
As usual, proud,
Alone, aloof,
He'd brought his courage to the roof.
But now upon the wire and bar
An animal in fear he stood,
Devouring fire in his wood
And at his feet a pit of tar.

His act? To somersault through air
Once twice thrice and burst
Through a red paper square.
Oh Jack be nimble, Jack be quick,
Your thin air grows dark and thick.
He took one last impure breath,
Balancing how a flier dies.
Then he left the bar, and then
Once
            twice
                    thrice.

side show:

Anger, the old tattoo,
Flooded his heart,

Rivered his veins,
And rivaled all the blue man's art.

Courage, the old measure,
Knew its pleasure,
Dwarfed the tall man, tripped him up.

Fear, the black barbell,
Fell. In that thunder
The strong man weakened and went under.

Then Fate, the lucky hick,
Swept the arcade:
Knocked down bottles, rang the bell,
Guessed each man's weight, and the right shell,
Saw through the skin show, did so well
He won all prizes. Quick,
He took his pick.

toward the destruction of elegy:

Small stones. As if the measurement of death
Consisted of some marble magnitude.
But better this for monument than crude
Trapping on a page with a black breath.
That could turn the sourest tongue more sour.
To see thought stiffen and contort can be
Too excellent a reminder of an hour
Already rendered much too readily.

Small stones. This deep remove
No man can quarry and no word can prove.
If all the answers tendered and applied
Curved firm containers for the tears we've cried . . .
But no schemes from philosophies apply.
A child has fashioned no pat way to die.

toward the destruction of luxury:

To lose what we had learned from what we saw
We sift through rubble for an unburnt straw,
But there are none. No, we had never guessed
Our civilization weak as all the rest;
We had built on sand on purpose, we
Used insubstantial fabric to keep free,
To stay precarious. That was the key,
We thought. Spend life within our lavish tents
And raise illusion through extravagance.

But ropewalkers had flipping hearts. Too bad.
Our clowns were wept and giggled out. Too bad.
The trainers had not tamed themselves. Too bad.
We should have known it of a canvas town.
It is a short time till the show's torn down.

Warning

April May June doesn't matter
Here much. The sameness
Outside, the similar months,
Slowly outwit Darwin and shape
The innards. The night sky fills
With words. It seems everyone is
Advertising.

The tourists make little
Of it. They expect strangeness
From any foreign city and are used
To adjusting.

At five, after the beach, the white
Clouds darken and there is rain.
Over our liquor we watch it
Fall. Almost time to shower again
And dress for dinner.

Far out above the sea a yellow
Bolt jags to the water. It
Is so far away not even it
Startles. Don't stay too long.

We say you get sand in your shoes.

Even America

Rust is at
My car

Mist from the sea
Certainly

The welcome light
At the front
Out

The bulb probably

Now the typewriter growls
In its bearings

I understand even America
Suspects its innards

So travel ends
So close neighbors
Stay away

I have had enough friends
And other foreign places

If new flames arise
Alive from the old fire

We'll keep dry
And lucky

We got it all in

On the Patio

An ant riot
At the coffeecup

A whole rimful of runners

It has got so one
Ought not put anything down

In fact they act as if
This the last taste of sweet

In their world

Enough to panic over

An ant economist might add two
And two together and figure

Another run on supply

See his society behave
Like no tomorrow

Were there a way
I would offer God knows
Tomorrow will see Him here

As usual
Leaning back thoughtful

For He remembers even
Yesterday

The Tanks of Amherst

The twin Cadillac engines roared
To my foot, while above
The turret whined electric,
Pointing the cannon over the pond.

Two girls ran to us from Memorial Hall,
Carrying sandwiches. We yawned
A hatch and they clambered in.

A joyride.

Up highway one sixteen toward Mount
Sugarloaf we clattered, then
Off the paved road up the hill
Under the apple trees, the
Experimental trees with grafted
Fruits from hybrid blossoms.

We chose the Delicious.

It was between wars. We shut
Down the engines and sunned
In the weak Spring shine,
Reserve officers training.

Later we rolled the great green
Thing next to the main road
To track the cannon on passing cars,
Fun to watch the fearful civilian
Faces under our power. With clear
Periscopes, we looked far

Into the distance.

Today, another war has ended.
The night news shows rows of tanks
Hard beside foreign highways,
Empty hulls, cannon askew.

At home, relaxed, once again
The nation rests between actions.
The trees that bred true, bud.
Summer is about to bloom.

Peace will cover the apples.

The Collected Me

The Miami Herald has arrived
Too late to do any good.
From here disaster is trivial
And too far away, opinion
Already becoming brittle.
I am not ready for today,

Neither. Back in the studio,
I gather my old poems about me.
I could make a suit of them
And do a wild little dance,
But somehow I am not ready for
Collection and publication,

Neither. What is this
Being trapped in the morning?
After toast, before coffee.
Even the weather in the west
Seems only impending. No,
There is no sense in the moment,

Neither. The newsboys are now
Way up the street with their
Burdens. The mailmen have yet
To order their day together.
Between is the word for it.
A blank flyleaf between covers.

Tomorrow, I promise, I will
Gather my wits and sort out
The rubbish, staple the good
Times, discard the trash.
I may even search out the
Meaning of history. Tomorrow.

A Bare Walk

She goes

To the garden every day
Though no roses bloom
At this shade of year

Though these seasons
The world is brown leaf
And black thorn she goes

The world will turn
And longstem tea and climber
Rose will turn

To color of old flame
And fire with scents of old
And green wood smoking

For the rose has learned
To last through its own burning
Of slow summer and flash
Blazes so

Since she has learned
A sister glow
And burn she goes
To the garden

If all past autumns teach
The leaf were learned
At root and taught to turn
Of petal she would go

And winter

Movements

for Jules Pagano

On the ride to the airport
All the young men were silent
Fidgeting thick buckles
Fingering straps
Some mumbled prayers
Doing a clumsy pennance perhaps

Inside the aircraft more silence
Deeper and more still
As if a storm gathered
Under the engines thunder

A moment in the doorway to
Emptiness a pause
Then the long float
Of timelessness

In the truck back
Everyone talked a mile a minute
All telling all about the personal
Hands waving like little flags
Private fourths of July
Suddenly public and splendid

Later on in my life I raced
Automobiles around corners
As fast as I could and faster
Till one spun and the tires screamed
I would never catch up

And later I dared myself to solo
My own plane in the Arctic
Black mountains moving by in the night
With the soft glow of instruments
Feeling for signal direction

It is something about finding yourself
Alone on the rushing background
It is something about losing yourself
In your own wide pondering

And even now and here on this travel
Casting for orientation or fix of some
Incredible angle or curve or even
Hint of location

As I cascade down the language
Hunting the one spot solo only
Where the hunting rests and the hunter
Meets himself smiling and easy

Cavendish

Others saw water: lakes of blue and the blue
Green ocean charging in foam on the sand.
Water, they knew, was most of a man, but
Then Cavendish found Hydro-gen, making
From fire, water. Water became clear.

Pools under trees, fresh wells, most
All creation sang anew. Cavendish withdrew,
A shy man, fearful of womanly currents.

Shy to the point of dying. From his bed
He ordered the watchers away, choosing
His own company at the last. The
Better to reflect? Afraid of his sighs?

He should give all of us pause, this
Divider of seas greater than the dreams
Of Moses, testing, who knows, even Death.

Monday at the Airport

About to fly I pass some airport time
Digesting the science of the month
Where one practitioner discloses
The universe is mainly a charged gas
And tells me with I sense a grin
Things are hardly solid
Compared with the hearts of stars

I must confess I never knew
They had a heart oh let alone
The sweet green earth might not
Support our every step

That one fine day the smiling adventurer
might stride out his front door
And quite within the realm
Of possibility sink
Up to his knees in molecules
Stuck home forever

        Or worse
Two lovers just about to kiss
Would find they'd fallen through
Each other and what they posited
As terminal and stiff
Was insubstantial evanescence
Love a dream less real
Than life under anesthesia
And all their lies about how soft
The other quite come true

Oh my my flight's about to leave
Though now these second thoughts
Gather like Nimbus clouds

What if the air won't actually
Hold a poet up for long?

When I look inside there is no
Heart of a star and it has
Been proven time and again
Thinner stuff prevails

Well what if it won't?
My trusting nature will
Take a deep breath of a charged gas
And charge: let's make believe
For one more day and let's pretend
For one more trip we

Can pursue the usual as usual
Can navigate the normal normally
And I for one must once again confess
Putting my travel folders down
I never really considered the far stars
I never truly flew beyond the moon

Series

When Francois Vieta invented the unknown,
Saying for the first time, Let X
Equal it, oh, the mathematicians
Scurried smiling. Here was a tool.

And after Leibniz got busy with his binary,
Our machines gabbled, Oh one,
What do you know?

Now we confront irrational numbers.
The counters ask, How intense
Is this or that idea of infinity?

Somehow we seem no closer, if in fact
We are now almost to the last decimal.
History awaits a final name. Who's who
Will have nothing left to carry over?

Hand Calculator

Two, four, sixteen, two fifty six,
Six five five three six, and off
Scale, says my electronic mathbox.
I can't get that high by myself.
Things never have squared easy.

Five, says the right hand. Same
Here, says the left. Evidently
Hands knew number before the brain
Noticed. Like my calculator, it
Was built in. Living proof.

You have to hand it to the chromo-
Some. Not only has it hit
The right answer, but it shows
Its work. Look around at the
Classroom, by God, all earth and air.

On Instruments

by dial

The world on his windows changing,
The aviator corrects his blindness
With ever closer approximations
On space so perfect only radios
Define the course and curves
And even these bend imperfect.

No pilot holds his truth true
For more than divisions of instant
Where time itself is suspect,
Inconstants on a background
Inconceivable even to a heart
Keeping its own approximations.

He comes to love it. He can feel
Invisible wings holding. It
Registers fulfilment never
Absolute or ever completely
Rewarded or finished in anything
More than a nearness to plan.
Then, finally, the land.

He sips caffeine, shutting
His speeds down, relaxing as
Gauges leave his retinas,
After images subsiding, and
The quick math fades, too, as
Constants suitable only for this
Part of the whole route fade. The real

Turns real. A waitress smiles.
He finishes to leave again.

by bell

The meditator starts his journey
With a delicate thought touching
The bud of the navel, and knows
How the nut commands its leaves
To bush, how the circling flower
Explodes to small then larger fruit
Which fall to independence.

His travel begins in a double
Center revolving itself
And then the double doubles
Curves like planets take and suns
Swing out and away to courses
Forming arms of galaxies and
Clusters of fingers, orbits of eyes.

He comes to love it. He can feel
The mind turn softly about itself,
Tasting organ, blood, and gland.
The very brain doubles its halves.
Hands clap a together metaphor.
The toes tap iambic pleasures.

All without moving. Only attention
Bells, enclosing interiors,
Wheeling away from the center navel,
Each cell touched on the path,
Each vision visited, each
Tangent turned to expansion.

The man is spun, he knows. The world
Insides itself. He stays.

by shell

The double helix springs outward
And inward. Galaxies of cell
and sun unwind their helices.
And what towards? Both cell and sun
Are shell. The path is clear. Grow.

The traveler is water. It could
Be plasma, a cloud of molecules,
Flying universe of excited atoms
Spinning. Then man is hydrogen.

Spin out from the navel, spin
In from the stars, man is
Middling, the skin of the real.